WALLINGFORD RIEGGER

DANCE RHYTHMS

FOR BAND

OPUS 58a

This band version, arranged by the composer, is based on the original orchestra version, Op. 58.

CONCERT BAND

Full Score
Condensed Score
C Piccolo
[2] 1st Flute
[2] 2nd Flute
[2] 1st & 2nd Oboes
English Horn
[2] 1st & 2nd Bassoons
E♭ Clarinet
[3] 1st B♭ Clarinet
[3] 2nd B♭ Clarinet
[3] 3rd B♭ Clarinet
E♭ Alto Clarinet
B♭ Bass Clarinet
1st E♭ Alto Saxophone
2nd E♭ Alto Saxophone
B♭ Tenor Saxophone
E♭ Baritone Saxophone

[3] 1st B♭ Cornet
[3] 2nd B♭ Cornet
[2] 3rd B♭ Cornet
[2] 1st B♭ Trumpet
2nd B♭ Trumpet
[2] 1st & 2nd Horns in F
[2] 3rd & 4th Horns in F
[2] 1st Trombone
2nd Trombone
3rd Trombone
Baritone (Treble Clef)
Euphonium (Baritone in Bass Clef)
[4] Basses
String Bass
Timpani
Marimba-Xylophone
[3] Percussion
Side Drum, Bass Drum, Cymbals

Associated Music Publishers, Inc.

DISTRIBUTED BY

DANCE RHYTHMS
for Band

Wallingford Riegger
Opus 58a

9

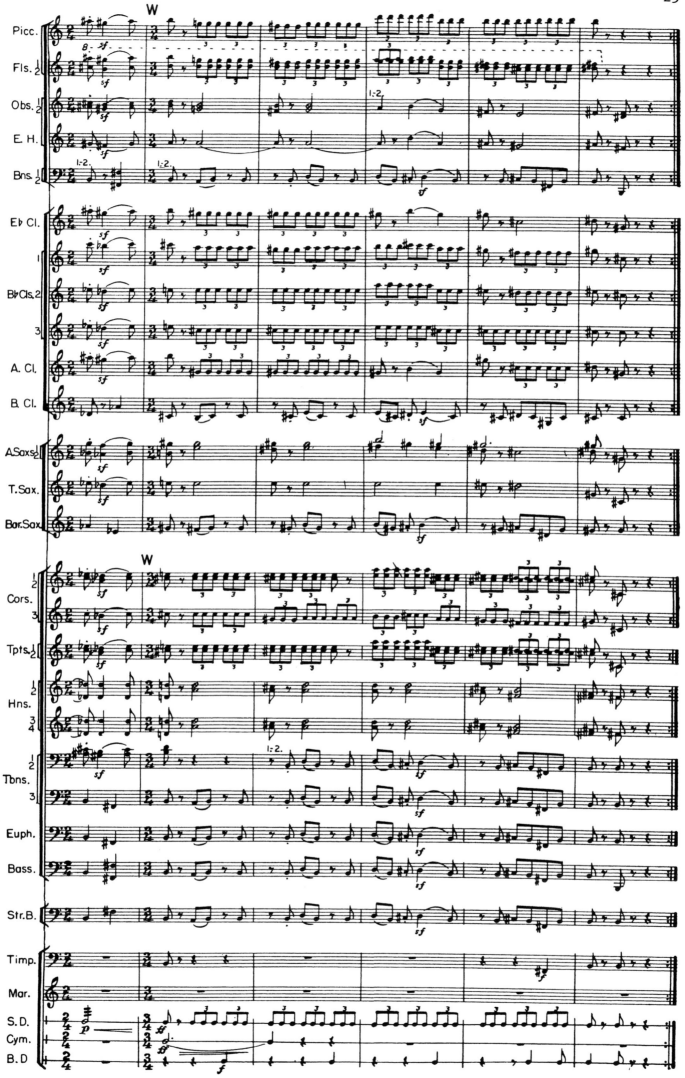

ISBN-13: 978-1-4803-4573-7

Distributed By

HAL LEONARD

50489898